My
Little House
Christmas Crafts Book

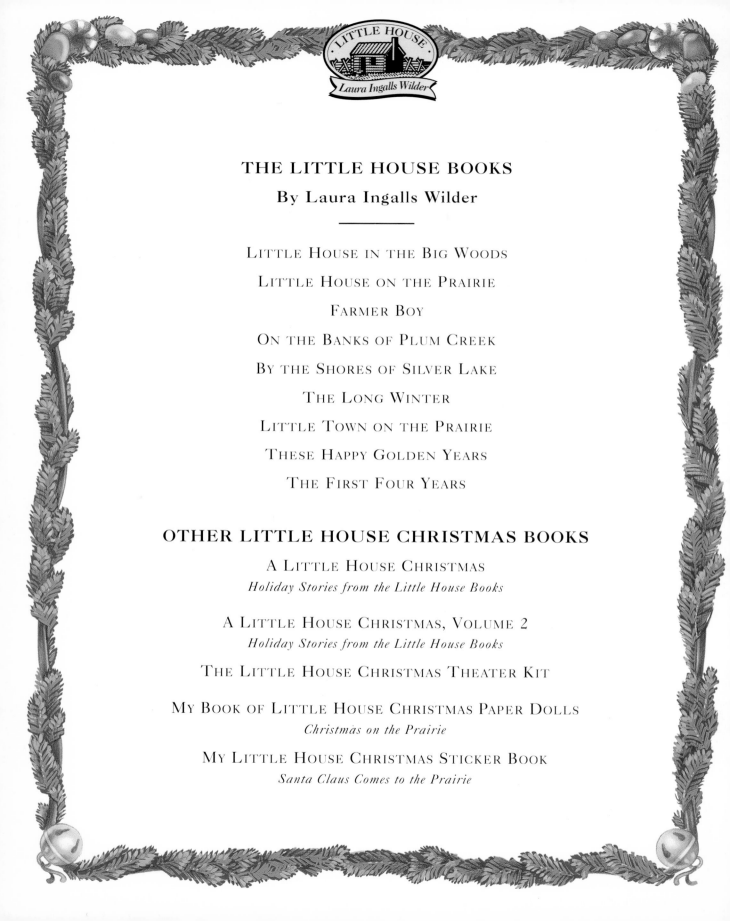

THE LITTLE HOUSE BOOKS
By Laura Ingalls Wilder

LITTLE HOUSE IN THE BIG WOODS

LITTLE HOUSE ON THE PRAIRIE

FARMER BOY

ON THE BANKS OF PLUM CREEK

BY THE SHORES OF SILVER LAKE

THE LONG WINTER

LITTLE TOWN ON THE PRAIRIE

THESE HAPPY GOLDEN YEARS

THE FIRST FOUR YEARS

OTHER LITTLE HOUSE CHRISTMAS BOOKS

A LITTLE HOUSE CHRISTMAS
Holiday Stories from the Little House Books

A LITTLE HOUSE CHRISTMAS, VOLUME 2
Holiday Stories from the Little House Books

THE LITTLE HOUSE CHRISTMAS THEATER KIT

MY BOOK OF LITTLE HOUSE CHRISTMAS PAPER DOLLS
Christmas on the Prairie

MY LITTLE HOUSE CHRISTMAS STICKER BOOK
Santa Claus Comes to the Prairie

LITTLE HOUSE

Laura Ingalls Wilder

My Little House Christmas Crafts Book

Christmas Decorations, Gifts, and Recipes
from the Little House Books

ILLUSTRATIONS BY *Mary Collier*
AND *Deborah Maze*

HarperFestival®
A Division of HarperCollins Publishers

"Red-and-White Striped Wrapping Paper,"
"Star-Edged Shelf Paper,""Ma's Clove Apple," "Popcorn Balls,"
"Laura's Heart-Shaped Cakes," and "Molasses-on-Snow Candy"
were written by Carolyn Strom Collins and Christina Wyss
Eriksson and illustrated by Deborah Maze. All previously
appeared in The World of Little House.

"Laura and Mary's Button String" was written by
Carolyn Strom Collins and Christina Wyss Eriksson.
"Aunt Eliza's Needlebook," "Mary's Braided Rug,"
"Carrie's Lace-Edged Handkerchief," and "Laura's Picture Frame"
were written by Margaret Irwin and illustrated by Mary Collier.
All previously appeared in My Little House Sewing Book.

"Pancake Men" was written by Amy Cotler and previously
appeared in My Little House Cookbook.

Contents

Little House
Christmas Decorations

*O*nce upon a time, a little girl named Laura Ingalls lived in a little log cabin in the Big Woods of Wisconsin with her Pa, her Ma, her big sister, Mary, and her baby sister, Carrie. Laura had many adventures as she traveled west across the prairie with her family in their covered wagon, and when Laura was grown, she wrote about of these adventures in the Little House books. Some of the most wonderful stories in these books are those that tell of the merry Christmas celebrations in the little houses. Because the Ingalls family didn't have much money, they didn't have many gifts or decorations, and their Christmas celebrations were always simple. Laura didn't see her first Christmas tree until she moved to Plum Creek, and sometimes there wasn't even very much food to eat on Christmas day. But Laura and her family, using readily available materials and a little imagination, were always able to make each Christmas a special one.

On the pages that follow you'll be able to share in Laura's Christmas celebrations by making some of the decorations, gifts, and foods she and her family made on the frontier. These crafts use just a few materials that you can buy at most sewing, craft, or even stationery stores. And in the Christmas crafts bag attached to the front of your book are many of the supplies you will need. Merry Christmas, Laura!

Plum Creek Popcorn Strings

When Laura popped corn, she would place the kernels in an iron kettle and set the kettle into a hole in the stove top. Occasionally she stirred the kernels with a long-handled spoon, but she had to be careful not to keep the lid off for too long; otherwise the corn would pop onto the floor!

To make popcorn strings, you will need:

freshly popped popcorn   *gold thread (in your Christmas*
needle with a small eye   *crafts bag)*
                                              scissors

1. With the scissors, cut a piece of thread that is as long as the popcorn string you want to make.

2. Make a double knot at one end of the thread, and thread the needle.

3. Push the needle carefully through the center of a piece of popcorn.

4. Gently push the piece of popcorn to the bottom of the thread with your fingers. If the popcorn breaks apart as you thread it, just use another piece.

5. Repeat with more popcorn until your string is full.

6. Remove the needle, and tie a double knot in the string. Drape the popcorn string on the branches of your Christmas tree or any other place you want to decorate.

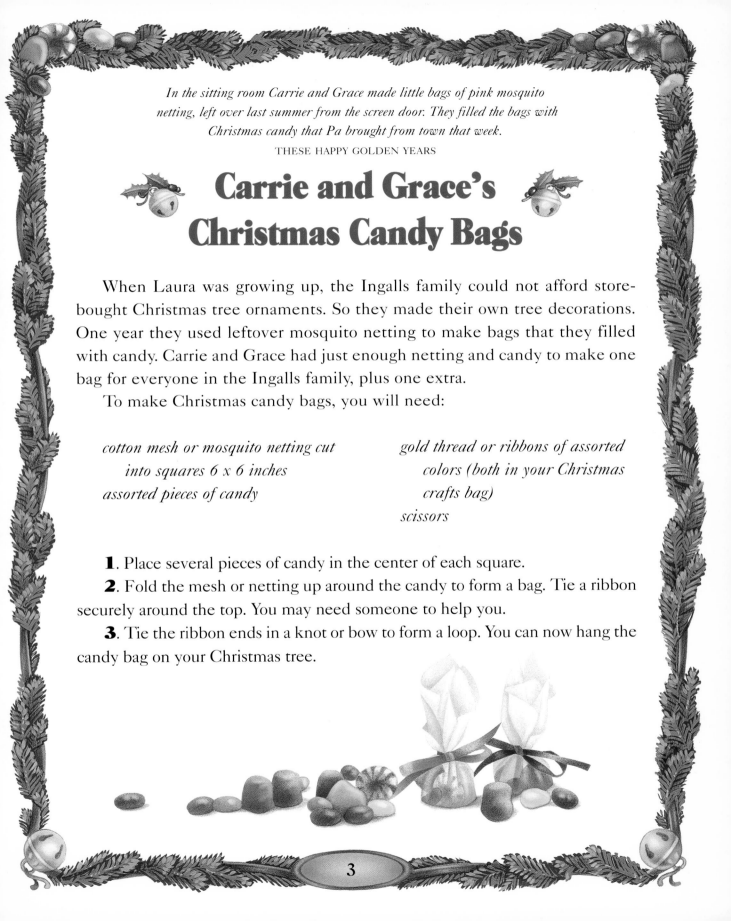

Carrie and Grace's Christmas Candy Bags

When Laura was growing up, the Ingalls family could not afford store-bought Christmas tree ornaments. So they made their own tree decorations. One year they used leftover mosquito netting to make bags that they filled with candy. Carrie and Grace had just enough netting and candy to make one bag for everyone in the Ingalls family, plus one extra.

To make Christmas candy bags, you will need:

cotton mesh or mosquito netting cut into squares 6 x 6 inches
assorted pieces of candy

gold thread or ribbons of assorted colors (both in your Christmas crafts bag)
scissors

1. Place several pieces of candy in the center of each square.

2. Fold the mesh or netting up around the candy to form a bag. Tie a ribbon securely around the top. You may need someone to help you.

3. Tie the ribbon ends in a knot or bow to form a loop. You can now hang the candy bag on your Christmas tree.

*The sleigh bells were ringing, the sleigh runners squeaking on the hard-
packed snow, and Laura was so happy that she had to sing.
"Jingle bells, jingle bells, | Jingle all the way!
Oh what fun it is to ride | In a one-horse open sleigh."*

THESE HAPPY GOLDEN YEARS

Almanzo's Jingle Bells

Almanzo tied little bells to his sleigh, so that whenever he went sleigh-riding with Laura, the bells would jingle and chime and make a pretty sound as they skimmed across the frozen prairie.

To make jingle bells, you will need:

*6 2-inch bells with hoops (available
    at craft stores)*

*piece of cotton string or satin
    ribbon, 30 inches long*

1. Slide a bell on one end of the string or ribbon.

2. Make a knot around the hoop to hold the bell in place.

3. Slide another bell on the string or ribbon about 4 inches away from the first bell, and make a knot.

4. Repeat until all the bells are tied on. Try to space them as evenly as possible.

5. Tie your jingle bell string to a door handle so that the bells will chime each time the door is opened. You can make your jingle bell string longer or shorter, or use different size bells if you like.

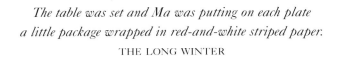

Red-and-White Striped Wrapping Paper

To make them look special, Ma wrapped her Christmas gifts in gift-wrap paper she may have made herself.

To make red-and-white striped wrapping paper, you will need:

newspapers
small disposable dish
1 jar of red acrylic paint

water
piece of cotton string, 36 inches long
large sheets of plain white paper

1. Spread newspapers on a flat work surface to protect it.

2. Pour some red paint into the disposable dish; add water to thin it down.

3. Dip the piece of string into the paint to coat it thoroughly.

4. Carefully remove the string from the paint. Holding each end of the string, lay the string down on the paper.

5. Make another stripe about an inch from the first one and continue across the whole width of the paper.

6. Dip the string in the paint again as needed.

7. Let the paper dry before wrapping gifts. You can use the paint-soaked string to tie up your package if you like.

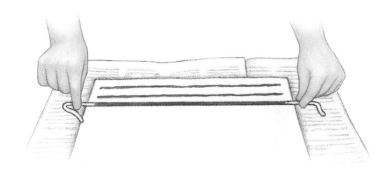

Standing in front of the crowded benches was a tree.
Laura decided it must be a tree. She could see its trunk and branches.
But she had never before seen such a tree. Where leaves would
be in summer, there were clusters and streamers of thin green paper.
ON THE BANKS OF PLUM CREEK

Christmas Tree Paper Streamers

One night, Ma and Pa packed the girls in the wagon and drove to town. When they walked into church, Laura was amazed to see a Christmas tree. She had never seen a Christmas tree before, and she hadn't even known it was Christmas!

The Christmas tree Laura saw was not like Christmas trees we have today. There were no evergreens on the prairie when Laura lived there; in fact, there were hardly any trees at all. So, for Christmas trees, people cut down small trees whose leaves had fallen off during the autumn, and decorated them with popcorn string, ribbons, and colored paper streamers.

To make paper streamers, you will need:

shiny foil paper (in your Christmas crafts bag) or construction paper of assorted colors
scissors

hole punch
gold thread (in your Christmas crafts bag)
pencil (optional)

1. Cut the paper into circles of all different sizes.

2. Make a small cut in the circle and cut in spirals toward the center of the circle. You can draw a cutting line on the circle with a pencil if you like.

3. Punch a hole in one end of the spiral paper streamer.

4. Thread a piece of the thread through the hole and tie onto your Christmas tree or any other place you want to decorate.

Ma showed Mary and Laura how to cut tiny bits out of the folded paper with the scissors. When each unfolded her paper, there was a row of stars. Ma spread the paper on the shelves behind the stove. The stars hung over the edges of the shelves, and the light shone through them.

ON THE BANKS OF PLUM CREEK

Star-Edged Shelf Paper

Ma made shelf paper to cover up unpainted wooden shelves. You can make Ma's shelf paper to decorate your room or house during Christmas, especially if you use shiny foil paper.

To make star-edged shelf paper, you will need:

green and red foil paper or construction paper	*pencil*
	scissors

1. Make sure your paper is wide enough to hang over the edge of your shelf, and make sure it is as long as the shelf. Tape pieces of paper together if you need to.

2. Fold the strip of paper into ½-inch accordion pleats.

3. Cut out pieces according to the diagram. Carefully unfold the paper and smooth it out.

4. Fold the edge with the stars down so that the stars hang down over the edge of the shelf. Secure the paper on the shelf with pieces of tape if you want to.

Little House Christmas Gifts

*L*aura grew up in a time and a place where virtually everything had to be made by hand. Laura and her family grew and prepared all their own food, made their own clothes, and even built the houses they lived in. And come Christmas time, they also made most of their own Christmas gifts. Because they lived in little houses, it was hard to keep the gifts a secret, but somehow they always managed.

On the following pages are six Little House gifts that Laura and her family made for one another long ago. You can make them too. You'll be sharing a part of Laura's life as you make them, and you'll have some useful and beautiful gifts that your family and friends will cherish forever.

Ma gave Aunt Eliza a little needle-book she had made,
with bits of silk for covers and soft white flannel leaves into which to stick
the needles. The flannel would keep the needles from rusting.
LITTLE HOUSE IN THE BIG WOODS

 # Aunt Eliza's Needlebook

Laura's Aunt Eliza, who was Ma's sister, her husband, Uncle Peter, who was Pa's brother, and their children came to spend Christmas with Laura and her family in the Big Woods of Wisconsin. Ma's gift to Aunt Eliza was a hand-made needlebook for keeping her needles safe. In return, Aunt Eliza gave Ma a large red apple stuck full of cloves.

To make a needlebook, you will need:

4 x 6 inch piece of satin or calico	*embroidery floss*
fabric	*needle (embroidery)*
4 x 6 inch piece of white flannel	*pins*
½ yard of ¼-inch-wide ribbon	*ruler*
scissors	*pencil*
poster board	*masking tape*
white paper	*glue or glue stick*

1. On your satin or calico fabric, use your ruler and pencil to draw a rectangle that measures 5¼ x 3½ inches. Cut out this rectangle of fabric, and fold the 5¼-inch side in half like a book. Crease the fold with your thumbnail. Unfold, and place the fabric, wrong side up, on a flat surface. With a ruler and a pencil, draw a line ⅛ inch from the center fold on each side.

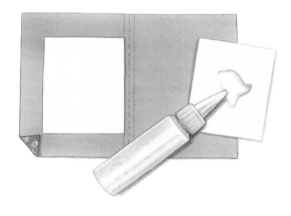

2. Cut out two rectangles of poster board, each measuring 2 x 2½ inches. Spread a thin coat of glue on one side of each rectangle. Place each rectangle, glue side down, on the wrong side of the fabric. Make sure each piece has one long edge on each line you drew on the fabric. There should be ¼ inch between the two pieces at the center fold and ½ inch of fabric outside the other three edges.

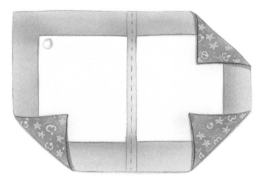

3. Put a dot of glue on each of the four outside corners of the poster board, and fold the fabric over the poster board to form triangles at the corners.

4. Put a thin line of glue along each of the three outside edges of each piece of poster board. Do not put glue along the center edges, since you will not be putting fabric there. Fold the fabric over the poster board along the top, bottom, and side edges, to glue in place.

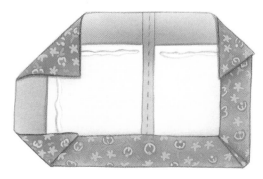

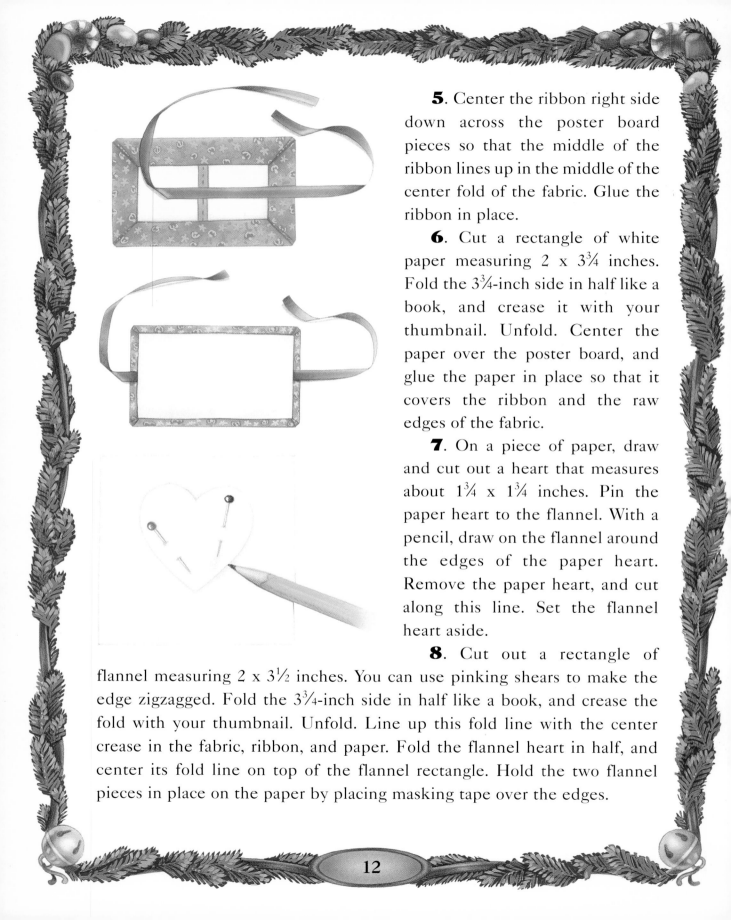

5. Center the ribbon right side down across the poster board pieces so that the middle of the ribbon lines up in the middle of the center fold of the fabric. Glue the ribbon in place.

6. Cut a rectangle of white paper measuring 2 x 3¾ inches. Fold the 3¾-inch side in half like a book, and crease it with your thumbnail. Unfold. Center the paper over the poster board, and glue the paper in place so that it covers the ribbon and the raw edges of the fabric.

7. On a piece of paper, draw and cut out a heart that measures about 1¾ x 1¾ inches. Pin the paper heart to the flannel. With a pencil, draw on the flannel around the edges of the paper heart. Remove the paper heart, and cut along this line. Set the flannel heart aside.

8. Cut out a rectangle of flannel measuring 2 x 3½ inches. You can use pinking shears to make the edge zigzagged. Fold the 3¾-inch side in half like a book, and crease the fold with your thumbnail. Unfold. Line up this fold line with the center crease in the fabric, ribbon, and paper. Fold the flannel heart in half, and center its fold line on top of the flannel rectangle. Hold the two flannel pieces in place on the paper by placing masking tape over the edges.

9. Cut an 18-inch piece of embroidery floss. Split the floss to two sections of three strands each. Thread the needle with one three-strand piece, and tie a beginning knot. Carefully lift the edge of the paper at the center fold line. Push the needle up through the paper close to the edge to hide the beginning knot under it. Make a backstitch over the edge of the paper. With a running stitch, sew through the layers of the flannel, paper, and fabric along the center line. Make an ending knot. Guide the needle under the top layer of fabric, close to the knot, and bring the needle tip up ¼ inch away. Cut the floss close to the fabric surface. This will hide the floss end.

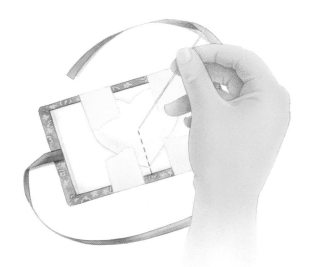

10. Fold your needlebook, and tie the ribbon in a bow to close. Push needles (and pins, if you like) through the flannel leaves of the needlebook for safekeeping.

Aunt Eliza had brought Ma a large red apple stuck full of cloves.
How good it smelled! And it would not spoil, for so many
cloves would keep it sound and sweet.

LITTLE HOUSE IN THE BIG WOODS

 # Ma's Clove Apple

Aunt Eliza was Ma's sister, and her husband, Uncle Peter, was Pa's brother. They lived about twelve miles away in the Big Woods, and they came to celebrate Christmas at the little house. Aunt Eliza gave Ma a clove apple as a Christmas gift.

To make a clove apple, you will need:

1 large red apple, very firm
½ cup whole cloves
toothpick (optional)

1. Press the sharp point of each clove into the apple. Push it in until only the head of the clove shows. You may need a toothpick to help you get started.

2. Continue until the whole apple is covered with cloves. You can make some designs on the apple with the cloves.

3. To display your apple, place it on a dish or in a bowl out of direct sunlight. You can also make clove oranges and clove lemons the same way you make clove apples.

Mary was braiding a new rug. She had cut worn-out
woolen clothes in strips, and Ma had put each color in a separate box.
Mary kept the boxes in order and remembered where each color was.
She was braiding the rag-strips together in a long braid
that coiled down in a pile beside her chair. When she came to the end
of a strip, she chose the color she wanted and sewed it on. . . .
Laura sewed the rag braid into a round rug and laid it heavy over
Mary's lap so that Mary could see it with her fingers.
THE LONG WINTER

Mary's Braided Rug

Although Mary lost her sight when the Ingalls family lived on Plum Creek, her blindness did not prevent her from working with her hands. All through the long winter, she braided and sewed strips of old fabric together to make a rug. Mary worked even when the storms made it so dark that Laura could not sew. "I can see with my fingers," Mary said.

Depending on the length and width of your fabric strips, you can make braided rugs of all different sizes. The rug below will be the perfect size for a doll's house, or for putting under a lamp, a plant, or a hot serving dish.

To make a braided rug, you will need:

⅜ yard each of three calico fabrics	*4 clothespins*
(any small-patterned cotton)	*masking tape*
needle (sharps)	*scissors*
thread	*ruler*
pins	*pencil*

1. With a ruler and a pencil, measure and mark two pieces, each measuring 2 x 45 inches, on each of your three fabrics. Cut out all six pieces on the marked lines.

2. On the wrong side of one 2-inch end of each piece, mark a sewing line ¼ inch from the edge.

3. Place the marked 2-inch ends of two matching pieces of fabric right sides together. Match the marked sewing lines, and pin. Thread a needle, and make a beginning knot. With a running stitch, sew along the sewing line. Make an ending knot, and remove the pins.

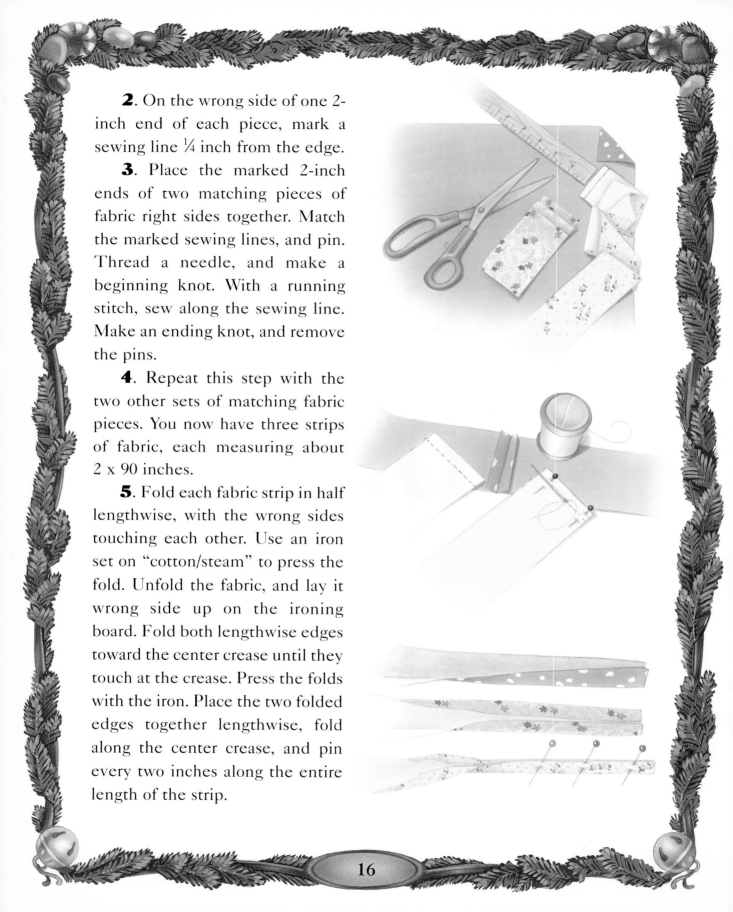

4. Repeat this step with the two other sets of matching fabric pieces. You now have three strips of fabric, each measuring about 2 x 90 inches.

5. Fold each fabric strip in half lengthwise, with the wrong sides touching each other. Use an iron set on "cotton/steam" to press the fold. Unfold the fabric, and lay it wrong side up on the ironing board. Fold both lengthwise edges toward the center crease until they touch at the crease. Press the folds with the iron. Place the two folded edges together lengthwise, fold along the center crease, and pin every two inches along the entire length of the strip.

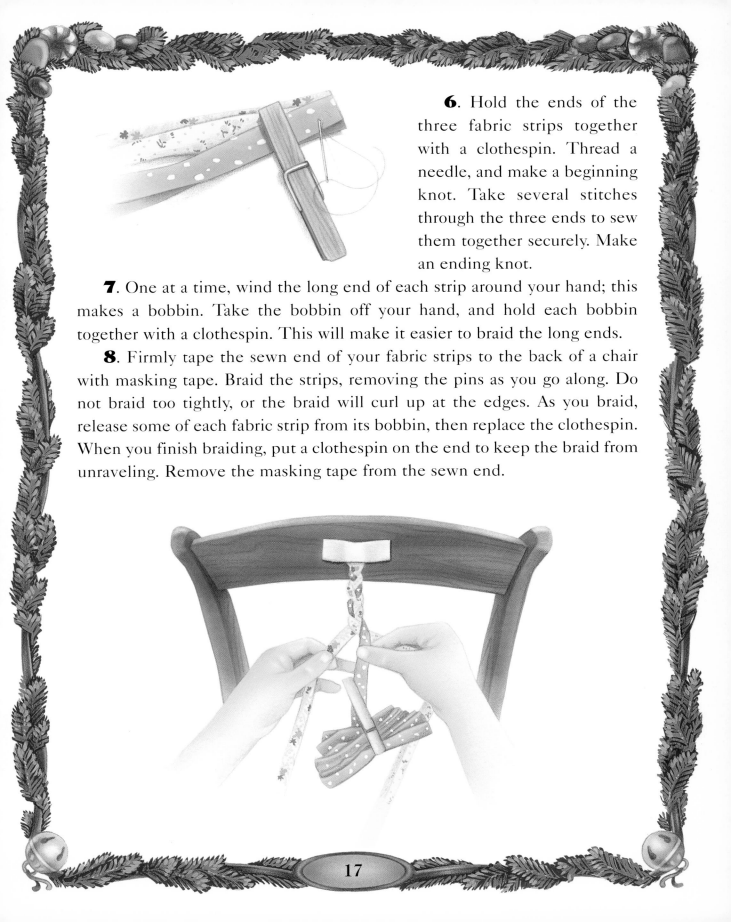

6. Hold the ends of the three fabric strips together with a clothespin. Thread a needle, and make a beginning knot. Take several stitches through the three ends to sew them together securely. Make an ending knot.

7. One at a time, wind the long end of each strip around your hand; this makes a bobbin. Take the bobbin off your hand, and hold each bobbin together with a clothespin. This will make it easier to braid the long ends.

8. Firmly tape the sewn end of your fabric strips to the back of a chair with masking tape. Braid the strips, removing the pins as you go along. Do not braid too tightly, or the braid will curl up at the edges. As you braid, release some of each fabric strip from its bobbin, then replace the clothespin. When you finish braiding, put a clothespin on the end to keep the braid from unraveling. Remove the masking tape from the sewn end.

9. Thread a needle, and make a beginning knot. Curve the sewn end of the braid around to the side and then behind the braid. Whipstitch the end of the braid to the back of the braid. On a flat surface, coil the braid in a circle and continue to whipstitch the side edges of the braid together. As you sew, make sure the braid lies flat and the stitches aren't too tight, or the rug will buckle when you are finished. Coil and sew until you are one inch from the end of the shortest fabric strip.

10. Cut the remaining fabric ends even, and pin them to the back of the rug (the side you have been sewing on). Sew the ends to the rug with a whipstitch. Make an ending knot, and remove the pins.

*The Christmas box had gone to Mary. In it Ma
carefully placed . . . the lace collar that she had knitted of finest
white sewing thread. Then she put in six handkerchiefs
that Carrie had made of thin lawn. Three were edged with narrow,
machine-made lace, and three were plainly hemmed.*
LITTLE TOWN ON THE PRAIRIE

Carrie's Lace-Edged Handkerchief

When Mary was at the school for the blind in Iowa, it was too expensive for her to return to Dakota Territory to spend Christmas with her family. So Pa, Ma, Laura, and Carrie carefully packed a Christmas box filled with their presents. In the box went a soft, woolen shawl Laura had crocheted, a lace collar, a blue ribbon Grace had bought, a five-dollar bill, a long letter they had all written, and six handkerchiefs. Christmas would not be the same without Mary, but when Mary received the box she would know that her family was thinking of her.

To make a lace-edged handkerchief, you will need:

⅜ yard of any white cotton fabric   *needle (sharps)*
    (lawn is very delicate and sheer   *pins*
    fabric)   *scissors*
1½ yards of ¾-inch-wide white   *ruler*
    ruffled lace trim   *pencil*
white thread

1. Lay out your fabric, right side down, on a flat surface. With a ruler and a pencil, measure and mark a 12-inch square. Cut out the fabric square on the marked line. Place the fabric square, right side down, on an ironing board.

Fold one edge over about ¼ inch toward the wrong side. Use an iron set on "cotton/steam" to press the fold. Repeat this step on the other three sides.

2. Fold over the folded edge another ¼ inch, and press with the iron as in Step 1. Pin the double-folded hem in place. Repeat this step on the other three sides, making sure the corners are neatly folded. Lay your fabric square, right side down, on a flat surface. You are now ready to pin on the lace.

3. The lace has a ruffled edge and a flat edge, and it has a right side and a wrong side. On the wrong side, the stitching is not as pretty and even as it is on the right side. Fold one cut end of the lace back ½ inch to the wrong side, and pin. Beginning at the center of one side of the fabric square, place the right side of the folded end of the lace on the wrong side of the fabric. Pin the flat edge of the lace to the double-folded edge of the fabric, so that the ruffled edge is outside the fabric square. After you have pinned them, check that the right sides of both the fabric and lace are on the other side.

4. Pin the lace to the double-folded edge of the fabric every inch along the sides. When you reach each corner, fold the lace to match the corner of the fabric, and pin it in place. When you have finished pinning the lace on all sides and are back to where you started, cut the lace so that the ends overlap ½ inch.

5. Thread a needle, and make a beginning knot. Slide the needle between the lace and the fabric to hide the knot. With a small and even running stitch, sew the lace to the fabric, removing the pins as you sew. You will be sewing through the lace and the double-folded hem at the same time. Make an ending knot on the wrong side of the handkerchief.

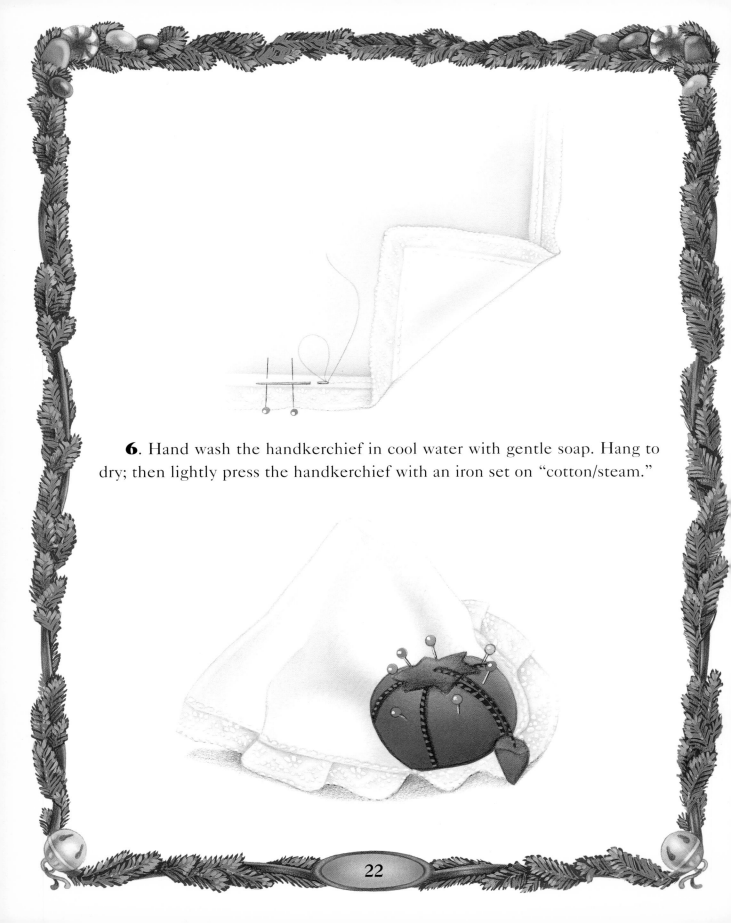

6. Hand wash the handkerchief in cool water with gentle soap. Hang to dry; then lightly press the handkerchief with an iron set on "cotton/steam."

Laura was making a little picture frame of cross-stitch
in wools on thin, silver-colored cardboard. Up the sides and across the top
she had made a pattern of small blue flowers and green leaves.
Now she was outlining the picture-opening in blue. While she put the tiny needle
through the perforations in the cardboard and drew the fine, colored
wool carefully after it, she was thinking how wistfully Carrie had looked at the
beautiful thing. She decided to give it to Carrie for Christmas.
Someday, perhaps, she could make another for herself.
THE LONG WINTER

Laura's Embroidered Picture Frame

When blizzard after blizzard forced the train across the prairie to stop running, all supplies were cut off for the families living in De Smet, South Dakota. Caught unprepared for Christmas, Laura decided to give Carrie a picture frame she had embroidered for herself. In May, when the train finally arrived with the Christmas barrel from Reverend Alden, it was full of wonderful gifts, including two boxes full of bright colored yarns, embroidery silks, and sheets of silver and gold perforated cardboard that Ma gave to Laura.

To make an embroidered picture frame, you will need:

crewel wool or embroidery floss   *glue*
    (blue, yellow, and green)   *ruler*
perforated paper (14 holes per   *pencil*
    inch)   *white poster board*
needle (tapestry or embroidery)   *needle threader*
small sharp-pointed scissors

1. On the back side of the perforated paper, use a pencil to mark a hole to be the starting point. Counting this hole as hole number 1, count 45 more holes across, and mark the ending point in hole number 46. With a ruler and a pencil, draw a line through the row of holes from hole number 1 to hole number 46. This line will measure about $3\frac{1}{8}$ inches. Beginning at hole number 1, count 51 holes down, and use a pencil to place a mark in hole number 52. With a ruler and a pencil, draw a line that connects hole number 1 and hole number 52. This line will measure about $3\frac{1}{2}$ inches. Repeat these directions to draw two more lines to form a rectangle, 46 holes across and 52 holes down. Cut out the rectangle on the marked lines. You how have a rectangle with 44 holes across and 50 holes down to stitch in.

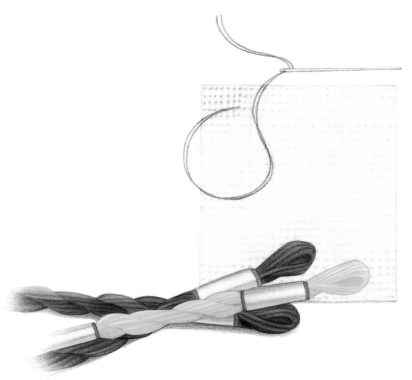

2. Thread a needle with two strands of blue crewel yarn (or three strands of embroidery floss) 24 inches long. Pull the yarn through the eye of the needle, leaving one end longer than the other. Do not make a beginning knot.

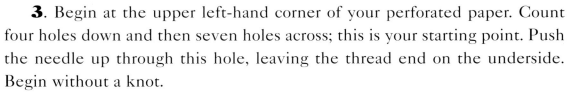

3. Begin at the upper left-hand corner of your perforated paper. Count four holes down and then seven holes across; this is your starting point. Push the needle up through this hole, leaving the thread end on the underside. Begin without a knot.

4. Sew with cross-stitches, following the Picture Frame Embroidery Chart. Each symbol on the chart represents a cross-stitch taken between four holes on the perforated paper. The different symbols represent different colors of floss or yarn. Stitch all the blue flowers first, then the green leaves, and finally the yellow centers. This will save you from having to thread the needle several times for each flower. If you make a mistake, simply unthread the needle and

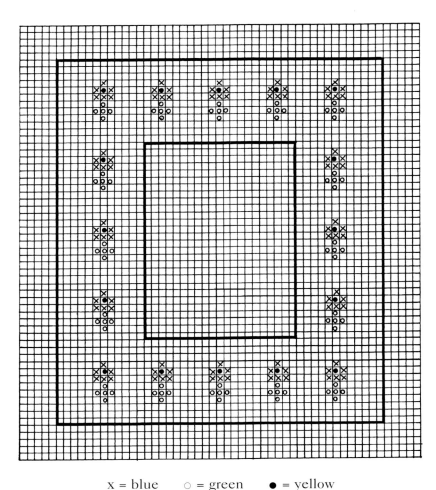

x = blue   o = green   ● = yellow

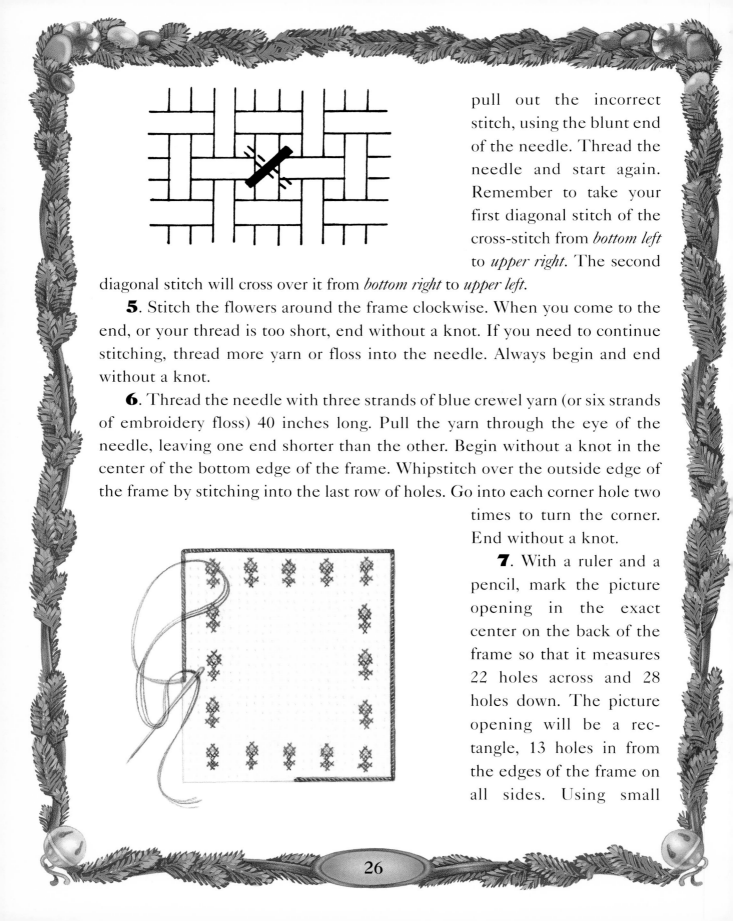

pull out the incorrect stitch, using the blunt end of the needle. Thread the needle and start again. Remember to take your first diagonal stitch of the cross-stitch from *bottom left* to *upper right*. The second diagonal stitch will cross over it from *bottom right* to *upper left*.

5. Stitch the flowers around the frame clockwise. When you come to the end, or your thread is too short, end without a knot. If you need to continue stitching, thread more yarn or floss into the needle. Always begin and end without a knot.

6. Thread the needle with three strands of blue crewel yarn (or six strands of embroidery floss) 40 inches long. Pull the yarn through the eye of the needle, leaving one end shorter than the other. Begin without a knot in the center of the bottom edge of the frame. Whipstitch over the outside edge of the frame by stitching into the last row of holes. Go into each corner hole two times to turn the corner. End without a knot.

7. With a ruler and a pencil, mark the picture opening in the exact center on the back of the frame so that it measures 22 holes across and 28 holes down. The picture opening will be a rectangle, 13 holes in from the edges of the frame on all sides. Using small

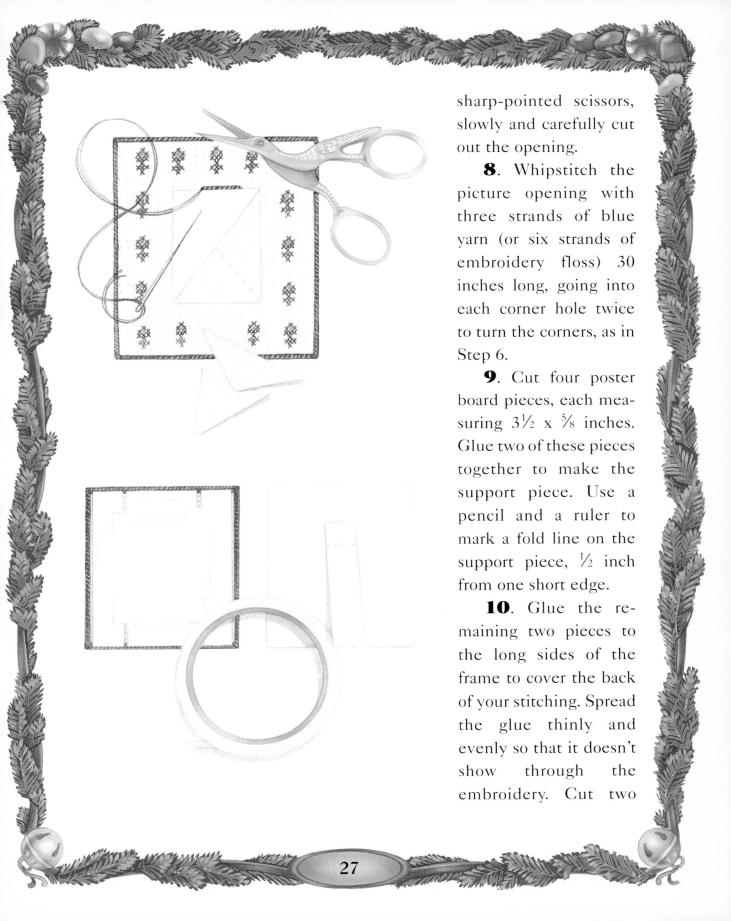

sharp-pointed scissors, slowly and carefully cut out the opening.

8. Whipstitch the picture opening with three strands of blue yarn (or six strands of embroidery floss) 30 inches long, going into each corner hole twice to turn the corners, as in Step 6.

9. Cut four poster board pieces, each measuring $3\frac{1}{2}$ x $\frac{5}{8}$ inches. Glue two of these pieces together to make the support piece. Use a pencil and a ruler to mark a fold line on the support piece, $\frac{1}{2}$ inch from one short edge.

10. Glue the remaining two pieces to the long sides of the frame to cover the back of your stitching. Spread the glue thinly and evenly so that it doesn't show through the embroidery. Cut two pieces of poster board, each measuring 1½ x ⅝ inches, and glue these carefully to cover the short sides of the frame. Let it dry.

11. Center a picture or a photograph behind the opening, and tape it in place. Make sure it is centered properly before you glue on the back in the next step.

12. Cut one rectangle of poster board to measure 3½ x 3⅛ inches. Spread the glue thinly and evenly along the back edges of this poster board. Center it over the back of the frame, and glue it on. Let it dry.

13. Position your support piece on the back of the frame, so that the unmarked short end is even with the bottom of the frame. With a pencil, draw a line on the back of the frame to mark where you will glue the support piece. Bend the support piece on its marked line. Spread glue on the ½-inch section, and glue it in place on the back of the frame. Let the glue dry before you stand up your picture frame.

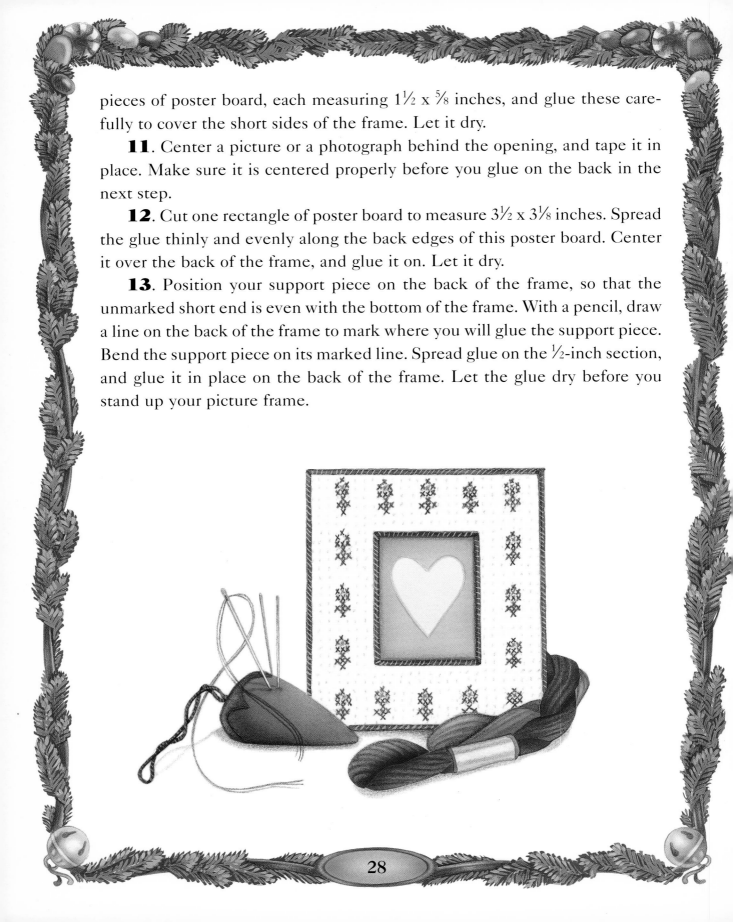

Ma beckoned Mary and Laura. Her face was shining with a secret.
They put their heads close to hers, and she told them.
They could make a button-string for
Carrie's Christmas!
ON THE BANKS OF PLUM CREEK

 # Laura and Mary's Button String

The first Christmas the Ingalls family spent on Plum Creek, there was very little money to buy gifts. But Ma thought of a present for Baby Carrie that would not cost anything and would be fun for Mary and Laura to make. It was a button string made from the buttons in Ma's button box. Ever since she was a little girl, Ma had saved buttons. She had silver- and gold-colored buttons, striped buttons, china buttons, and even one tiny dog-head button, and she kept them all in her button box. Mary and Laura spent evenings stringing the buttons and making "the most beautiful button-string in the world" for Carrie.

To make a button string, you will need:

lots of buttons of all shapes and   *gold thread, 9 to 12 inches long (in*
    colors (some buttons are in your   *your Christmas crafts bag)*
    Christmas crafts bag)   *an embroidery needle (optional)*

1. Double knot a small button to one end of the thread.

2. Slide buttons onto the thread, one at a time. To make it easier to string the buttons, you can stiffen the other end of the thread with a drop of glue or wax, or slip it through the eye of an embroidery needle. If you want to change the order of the buttons, just slip them off and begin again.

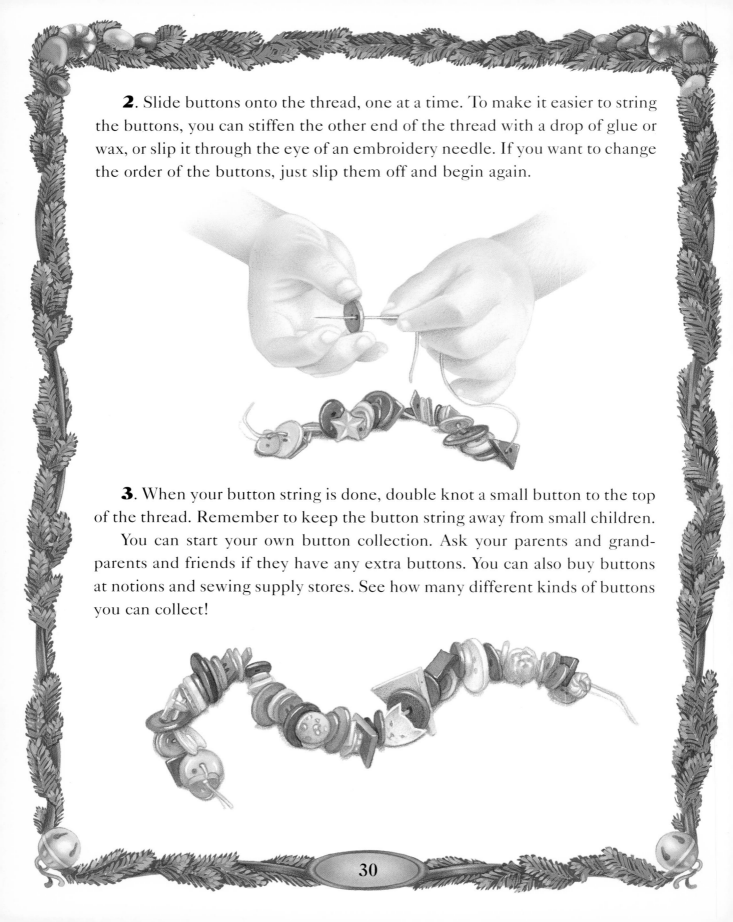

3. When your button string is done, double knot a small button to the top of the thread. Remember to keep the button string away from small children.

You can start your own button collection. Ask your parents and grandparents and friends if they have any extra buttons. You can also buy buttons at notions and sewing supply stores. See how many different kinds of buttons you can collect!

Little House Christmas Recipes

*T*hroughout the Little House books, Laura described the many kinds of frontier foods she prepared and ate as she was growing up. Some of the most memorable meals she described were the Christmas dinners when Ma always managed to come up with a surprise for the family. Even during the long, hard winter in Dakota Territory, when the Ingalls family had barely any food, Ma managed to make a delicious oyster soup. Most of the time, though, Christmas was a time when there was lots of food, from pancake men for breakfast to molasses-on-snow candy for dessert.

On the following pages are recipes for five of Laura's favorite Christmas foods. They are easy to follow and will bring a part of Laura's frontier experience to your own Christmas meals.

For breakfast there were pancakes,
and Ma made a pancake man for each one of the children.
It was exciting to watch her turn the whole
little man over, quickly and carefully, on a hot griddle.

LITTLE HOUSE IN THE BIG WOODS

 # Pancake Men

Laura and Mary's cousins, Alice and Ella and Peter, spent Christmas Eve and Christmas with the Ingalls family. On Christmas morning Ma made pancake men while all the children watched. Peter ate the head off his pancake man right away, but the four girls ate theirs slowly and saved the heads for last.

To make pancake men, you will need:

½ cup whole wheat flour
½ cup unbleached white flour
½ teaspoon baking soda
¼ teaspoon salt
2 tablespoons butter
1 egg

1 cup buttermilk
2 tablespoons maple syrup
oil or butter to cover pan
maple syrup and butter (or
other toppings of your choice)

1. Put dry ingredients in the medium bowl. Stir until mixed.

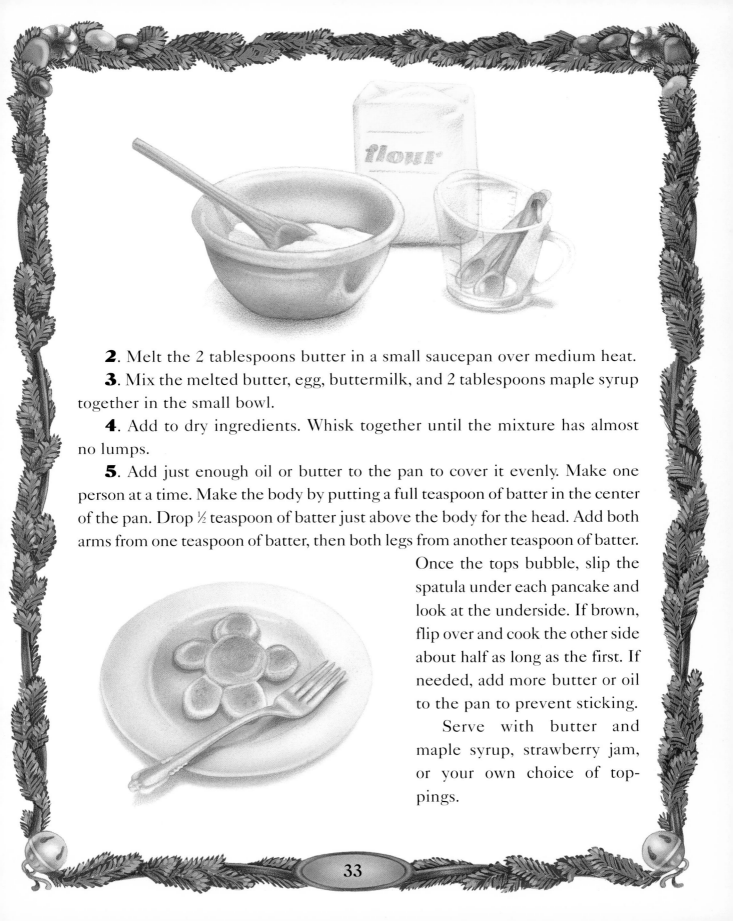

2. Melt the 2 tablespoons butter in a small saucepan over medium heat.

3. Mix the melted butter, egg, buttermilk, and 2 tablespoons maple syrup together in the small bowl.

4. Add to dry ingredients. Whisk together until the mixture has almost no lumps.

5. Add just enough oil or butter to the pan to cover it evenly. Make one person at a time. Make the body by putting a full teaspoon of batter in the center of the pan. Drop ½ teaspoon of batter just above the body for the head. Add both arms from one teaspoon of batter, then both legs from another teaspoon of batter. Once the tops bubble, slip the spatula under each pancake and look at the underside. If brown, flip over and cook the other side about half as long as the first. If needed, add more butter or oil to the pan to prevent sticking.

Serve with butter and maple syrup, strawberry jam, or your own choice of toppings.

When Laura's kettle was full of popped corn, Ma dipped some into a large pan,
poured a thin trickle of the boiling molasses over it, and then buttering her hands, she deftly
squeezed handfuls of it into popcorn balls. Laura kept popping corn and Ma made it
into balls until the large dishpan was heaped with their sweet crispness.

BY THE SHORES OF SILVER LAKE

Popcorn Balls

On Christmas Eve it began to snow, and Pa was afraid it would "turn into a blizzard." So instead of going to the church service in town, the Ingallses decided to celebrate Christmas Eve at home. They made popcorn balls, tied Christmas candy in pink mosquito netting bundles, and sang their favorite songs while Pa played the fiddle.

To make popcorn balls, you will need:

4 quarts popped corn   *large bowl*
½ cup molasses   *large saucepan*
2 cups brown sugar   *candy thermometer or cup of cold*
4 tablespoons butter   *water*
⅓ cup water   *mixing spoon*
butter for your hands   *waxed paper*
measuring cup and spoons

1. Pour the popcorn into a large bowl that leaves plenty of room for mixing.

2. Combine the molasses, brown sugar, butter, and water in the saucepan.

3. Bring this mixture to a boil, and keep it boiling over low to medium heat until it reaches 250° on the candy thermometer or until a few drops of it form a hard ball in cold water. This will take about 20 minutes.

4. Carefully pour the hot syrup over the popped corn, and mix it with a spoon. Set aside to cool at least 10 or 15 minutes.

5. Butter your hands well. When the popped corn mixture is cool enough to handle but still warm enough for the syrup to remain liquid, gather handfuls and press them lightly into balls about the size of tennis balls or baseballs. *Be very careful not to burn yourself! The molasses mixture can be extremely hot.*

6. Work quickly to keep from burning your hands, and keep buttering your hands to keep them from sticking to the popcorn balls.

7. Set the popcorn balls on waxed paper to harden.

Pile the popcorn balls in a big dish to enjoy right away, or wrap them in waxed paper or plastic wrap to keep for a day or two.

Mary and Laura pulled out two small packages.
They unwrapped them, and each found a little heart-shaped cake.
Over their delicate brown tops was sprinkled
white sugar. The sparkling grains lay like tiny drifts of snow.

LITTLE HOUSE ON THE PRAIRIE

Laura's Heart-Shaped Cakes

The Ingallses' neighbor, Mr. Edwards, swam across a rain-swollen creek in the freezing cold to bring Mary and Laura their presents from Santa Claus—shiny new tin cups, sticks of peppermint candy, a penny apiece, and delicate heart-shaped cakes. Laura and Mary thought the cakes were almost too pretty to eat.

To make heart-shaped cakes, you will need:

½ cup butter or margarine,
* softened*
2 tablespoons granulated sugar
¼ teaspoon vanilla
1¼ cups all-purpose flour
granulated sugar for sprinkling
measuring cup and spoons
large mixing bowl
mixing spoon

floured board
rolling pin (optional)
heart-shaped cookie cutter, about
* 2 x 3 inches across*
cookie sheet
pot holder
wide spatula
wire rack

1. Preheat the oven to 325°.

2. Beat the butter, sugar, and vanilla together until the mixture is light and fluffy.

3. Stir in the flour.

4. On a floured board, pat or roll the dough out into a circle about ⅓ inch thick.

5. Cut out shapes with the cookie cutter.

6. Gather the leftover scraps into a ball. Pat or roll the ball into a circle, and cut more cakes.

7. Sprinkle the tops of the cakes with granulated sugar.

8. Put the cakes on the cookie sheet and bake them for about 15 to 20 minutes, until they are lightly browned.

9. Take the cakes out of the oven and sprinkle more granulated sugar on the tops.

10. Carefully remove the cakes with a spatula to a wire rack to cool. This recipe makes about 12 heart-shaped cakes.

*Almanzo couldn't help gazing at the triangles of pie, waiting
by his plate; the spicy pumpkin pie, the melting cream pie, the rich, dark mince
oozing from between the mince pie's flaky crusts.*

FARMER BOY

Mother Wilder's Christmas Mincemeat Pie

Mincemeat pie was one of Almanzo's favorite kinds of pies. It was made of the best bits of beef, chopped or minced very fine, raisins, spices, sugar, and chopped apples. Almanzo's mother would boil the beef first, chop it fine, and then mix in the rest of the ingredients. Then she would pack it in jars, where it would keep until she wanted to make a pie. She let Almanzo eat the scraps left in the bowl.

Nowadays, you can buy prepared mincemeat, and some kinds don't even have any meat in them! Below is a simple meatless "mincemeat" mixture for an easy and delicious version of mincemeat pie.

To make mincemeat pie, you will need:

*9-inch prepared pie crust
   (available in grocery stores)
1½ cups seedless raisins
4 tart apples, peeled and cored
½ orange, including rind
½ lemon, including rind*

*½ cup cider vinegar
1½ cups dark-brown sugar
½ teaspoon salt
½ teaspoon cinnamon
½ teaspoon nutmeg
½ teaspoon ground cloves*

1. Preheat the oven to 425°.

2. Lay the pie crust in a 9-inch pie pan. Prick the dough all over with a fork and bake for 10 to 15 minutes. Remove crust from oven.

3. Coarsely chop the raisins, apples, orange, and lemon. Put mixture in saucepan.

4. Add the vinegar and heat just until the mixture boils. Reduce the heat and simmer for 10 minutes.

5. Add the sugar and spices and simmer 15 minutes more.

6. Remove from heat and let cool.

7. Fill the pie shell with the mixture. Serve at room temperature or reheat for 10 minutes in a warm oven. You can serve the pie with whipped cream if you like.

One morning Ma boiled molasses and sugar together until they made a thick syrup, and Pa brought in two pans of clean, white snow from outdoors. Laura and Mary each had a pan, and Pa and Ma showed them how to pour the dark syrup in little streams onto the snow. They made circles, and curlicues, and squiggledy things, and these hardened at once and were candy.

LITTLE HOUSE IN THE BIG WOODS

 # Molasses-on-Snow Candy

Before Christmas, Ma spent many hours making good things to eat, including molasses-on-snow candy. Laura and Mary helped Ma make the candy and were allowed to eat one piece each. The rest they saved for Christmas Day, when Aunt Eliza, Uncle Peter, and the cousins came to visit.

To make molasses-on-snow candy, you will need:

1 cup molasses
1 cup brown sugar
fresh, clean snow (or finely
   crushed ice)
measuring cup
large pot

spoon
candy thermometer or cup of
   cold water
shallow pan about 9 x 13 inches
clean tea towel or waxed paper

1. Mix the molasses and sugar together in the large pot and boil until the mixture reaches the "hard crack" stage on the thermometer or until a drop of the mixture dropped into the cold water forms a hard ball and cracks.

2. Remove the syrup from the heat. *Be careful—the syrup is very, very hot!*

3. Scoop fresh, clean snow into the shallow pan. You can also use finely crushed ice instead of snow.

4. Dribble a spoonful of syrup onto the snow or ice in "circles, and curlicues, and squiggledy things." Make lots of different shapes.

5. When the syrup turns hard and becomes candy, lift it off the snow and place it on the tea towel or waxed paper to dry.

 Index